Southern
Ghosts

Southern Ghosts

by
Nancy Roberts

SANDLAPPER PUBLISHING CO., INC.
Orangeburg, South Carolina

Sixth Printing 1996

First published by Doubleday and Company, Inc.
This edition published by Sandlapper Publishing Co., Inc.
Orangeburg, SC 29115

Manufactured in the United States of America

Photographs by Bruce Roberts

Library of Congress Cataloging-in-Publication Data

Roberts, Nancy, 1924–
    Southern ghosts.

    Summary: Presents thirteen accounts of apparitions and hauntings in the South.
    1. Ghosts—Southern States—Juvenile literature.
(1. Ghosts—Southern States) I. Title.
BF1472.U6R64   1987   133.1'0975   86-21955
ISBN 0-87844-075-5 (soft)

Contents

Southern Ghosts

THE ETERNAL DINNER PARTY

On the outskirts of Savannah is a place full of mystery. Those who enter it at dusk and walk beneath the moss-draped branches of the gnarled old oaks will soon sense the companionship of spirits. For Bonaventure Cemetery, the resting place of the remains of thousands of the dead, is awesome indeed, when the sun goes down. To learn its secrets, by all means, tarry and listen.

On these grounds there was once a great mansion overlooking the Wilmington River. Its beautiful, terraced gardens stretched from the front of the house down to the very edge of the water. The elaborate home, built of bricks imported from England, was the gift of Col. John Mulryne to his daughter Mary, soon to be the bride of Josiah Tattnall.

The hundreds of live oaks whose twisting limbs form a canopy overhead were planted by the colonel in the pattern of an M entwined with a T. The young couple loved their home, which was called Bonaventure, but when the war with England began, Josiah Tattnall's loyalty to the king made him a marked man. Taking his wife and young son, he left for England.

The son loved his Georgia home, and during his days at Eton he determined to return and fight for the Patriots. Sailing back to Georgia he joined the forces of Nathaniel Greene.

Although Bonaventure had been confiscated by the Patriots, when the young heir returned and fought bravely in the struggle for independence, the Patriots gave him back his birthplace. It was here that he brought his bride, and they walked happily together beneath the magnificent oaks.

Josiah, Jr., was a brigadier general, a member of Congress, and eventually governor of Georgia. He and his wife were prominent in the social life of Savannah, entertaining neighbors from surrounding plantations at great banquets and parties. Some guests arrived by boat at the landing on the riverfront. Others, in fine carriages, drove up the curved roads beneath the oaks. The pleasant years wore on at

Bonaventure, and there was no indication of tragedy ahead.

It was late November when guests began to arrive for one of the most elaborate dinner parties ever to be held at the house. There were hams and turkeys, wild duck, oyster casseroles, imported wines and champagne. Servants had festooned the house with greenery from the gardens and lighted lanterns, which hung from the trees along the impressive avenue of oaks. In each room fireplaces gave forth a warm glow adding to the festive appearance, and many of the guests commented, "Bonaventure has never looked lovelier."

As the guests were enjoying the first course, the butler hurried into the dining room and whispered something to the host. Josiah Tattnall excused himself. In a few minutes he returned and said calmly, "Ladies and gentle-men, I apologize for a slight interruption. Please follow me out to the garden and we will continue our dinner there." Tattnall led his guests outside.

Much to everyone's amazement, servants began carrying chairs out to the garden, and shortly the table arrived with all the food in place. Then, Josiah Tattnall quietly announced,

"Bonaventure is on fire and will soon be destroyed by the flames. We are all quite safe and I would like for you to remain and enjoy your dinner." A servant asked if he should bring lamps or candles and Tattnall replied, "No, the flames from Bonaventure will illumine our table."

As the great house burned brightly, the guests feasted upon ham and roast duck and drank toasts to Bonaventure and its rich memories. When the dinner was over, Josiah Tattnall arose and lifted his glass in a toast. "May the joy of this occasion never end," said he. Then he shattered the empty crystal goblet against one of the great oaks. His guests drank with him, following his example and shattering their glasses against the trunks of the surrounding trees, as sparks from the mansion rose high in the air.

In the years that followed, the beautiful Bonaventure Plantation became a cemetery. Late at night passersby have sometimes been startled to hear sounds of a gay dinner party in progress—the chatter of voices and the tinkle of crystal glasses shattering as if struck against a tree.

Those who dared have paused and listened

Bonaventure Plantation became a cemetery.

and wondered that so many years later, not far from the graves of Josiah Tattnall and his family, peals of eerie laughter and the revelry of the eternal dinner party still ripple and rustle through the camellias and among the moss-shrouded branches of the live oaks.

PRESIDENT CARTER'S HAUNTED HOUSE

The children skipped and jostled each other as they walked down the road after school in the small community of Plains, Georgia.

"Who wants to go past the house alone?" they sometimes called out to each other. "Not me," would come back a chorus of voices.

"Should we go by it today or go through the woods?"

"Through the woods, the woods," they'd shout. And even on dark winter days they would run among the shadows of the tall pines down the brush-lined path where sweet gum branches sprang back and stung their faces. For the gloom of the forest was less frightening than the *haunted house*.

The house had been built in 1840, almost a century before a little girl named Rosalynn Smith gazed at it fearfully. Weeds had grown tall and ragged around it. The chimney careened at a crazy slant and shutters sagged half off their hinges beside windows staring out at the road with dark and hostile eyes.

Over the years a story was told in the neighborhood of how late at night in one of the windows a woman could be seen wearing a long white gown and holding a candle. This was just one of many stories.

In July 1946, Rosalynn married a young man from Plains named Jimmy Carter. On returning to Plains when Carter's military service was over, the couple could not find a place to live, for there were few houses available in the small town. In fact, at the time only one was for sale. It was the haunted house, the old place Rosalynn and all the children had often walked through the woods to avoid.

But Rosalynn put aside childish thoughts and fears. The house was small and just right for them at the time. It might even be fun to remodel for, after all, it did have a history, didn't it?

So, Rosalynn and Jimmy Carter had the floors repaired, the roof replaced, interior walls plastered and painted, the kitchen made modern and cozy, the old chimney carefully rebuilt, and the shutters painted and properly hung. There was enough of a din from the saws and hammers to chase even the most tenacious spirit right back where it came from.

Now there was real charm to the old place and the Carters felt they would enjoy it. Boxes were unpacked, crisp white curtains hung, and guests came bringing gifts for the housewarming. Some made smiling inquiries about the lady with the light, but no one had seen her. Evidently her candlelight vigil at the window had ceased.

A week later the Carters were seated in their living room when they heard a loud crash. They rushed up to the attic from whence the sound came. They were certain that it was the attic window that had been propped open, for it sounded as if the window had slammed down hard upon the sill. But when they reached the room and looked at the window, it was still propped up just as they had left it. Sometimes loud knocks or crashing sounds could be heard not only from the attic but also from the outside attic stairs. It often happened when the family was gathered at the dinner table, but no evidence could ever be found as to the cause.

A woman could be seen wearing a long white gown and holding a candle.

Neighbors reported seeing the light burning in the window of the room from which the sounds most frequently came. One story about the house was that the strange happenings there were due to the spirits of a Confederate soldier and his sweetheart who kept a candle burning for him at her window.

How did the Carters feel about all this? They say they rather enjoyed sharing the house with the ghosts.

THE VAN LANDINGHAM GHOST

Many of us believe that ghosts tend to avoid busy cities or that they appeared more often in the past than they do in the present. But nothing could be farther from the truth.

It was a sunny day in Charlotte, North Carolina, in the spring of 1976. The gardens of the old Van Landingham estate were an outburst of color erupting from a lawn still clad in patches of winter leaves.

A late afternoon wedding was to take place in an open area behind the house, and guests were settling themselves in rows of chairs under the shade of a giant oak. The groom's brother, who was an experienced photographer, shot pictures of the bridesmaids and preparations for the wedding. Now he turned his attention to the ceremony itself and focused his camera on the bridal pair and the minister.

As he tried to focus he found he was having difficulty. A fuzzy image kept appearing in his lens just at the moment he thought he had the couple and the minister in sharp focus. Ready to press the shutter, he would see a short man with reddish hair standing directly in front of the minister.

He peered in bewilderment through his lens. Each time he lowered the camera he would see there was no little man there, only three people—the bride, the groom, and the minister. Finally, he went ahead and shot the pictures.

This was not the only strange event of the wedding. Later, while the photographer stood taking pictures of the bride in the receiving line, he saw the minister come up to her.

"I want to apologize for such a short ceremony," he said. "I had placed my notes for the wedding service in my Bible, but somehow, just before I was to begin I found they had disappeared completely."

Gazing down the receiving line, the photographer noticed the grandfather of the groom, a very old man whose health was so poor it had been doubtful whether he would be able to attend the wedding at all. There seemed to

be something familiar about the old man and, with surprise, the photographer recognized the fuzzy figure that had appeared in his lens while he was taking pictures during the ceremony. It was the grandfather of the groom! His was the "image" seen in the lens.

The color film had to be sent off to be developed and the photographer could scarcely wait for it to come back. When it arrived he looked at each frame. Everything seemed to be just as it should. But deciding to go over it more carefully with his magnifying glass, he found two frames that filled him with astonishment and a kind of awe. For there was the image of a short, red-haired figure—the top of his head reaching the point of the minister's chin. It was the grandfather of the groom!

Two weeks after the wedding of his favorite grandson the old man died. How he became part of the wedding pictures will always remain a mystery. Psychologist Carl Jung had a theory that may shed some light upon it. Sometimes a person visualizes his own imminent death. Jung speaks of the foreknowledge of coming death as reflecting back from the future into the present moment.

We can only conjecture whether it is possible to have ghosts appear from the future as well as the past. The photographer's experience might seem to say yes.

THE BROWN MOUNTAIN LIGHTS

The Brown Mountain Lights have been described as a "troop of candle-bearing ghosts destined to march forever back and forth across the ridge of the mountain." They are one of North Carolina's most famous phenomena.

The lights first attracted the attention of German engineer Gerard William de Brahm, who saw them in 1771. He believed that the mountains emitted nitrous vapors that were borne by the wind, and when laden winds met each other the niter inflamed and deteriorated.

Early frontiersmen thought that the lights were the spirits of Catawba and Cherokee warriors slain in an ancient battle on the mountain. One thing is certain, the lights do exist. They have been investigated at least twice by the U.S. Geological Survey and have been reported many times in newspaper stories.

Appearing at irregular intervals over the

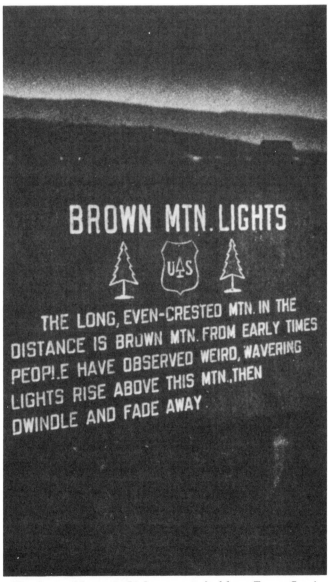

The Brown Mountain Lights are marked by a Forest Service sign.

top of Brown Mountain—a long, low mountain in the foothills of the Blue Ridge—they move erratically up and down, visible at a distance, but vanishing as one climbs the mountain. From Wiseman's View on Linville Mountain the lights can be seen well. They have a reddish or blue cast and at first they appear to be about twice the size of stars. On dark nights they sometimes rise so thick and fast it is impossible to count them.

The first scientific investigation was undertaken by the U. S. Geological Survey in 1913, and the conclusion reached was that the lights were locomotive headlights from the Catawba Valley to the south. But three years later when the great flood of 1916 swept through the valley, the railroad bridges were knocked out. It was weeks before the right-of-way could be repaired and the locomotives could once again enter the valley. Roads were washed away and power lines were down, but the lights continued to appear as usual and it was apparent they could not be reflections from locomotive or automobile headlights.

In the 1930s the *Guide to the Old North State*, prepared by the Works Progress Administration, stated that the Brown Mountain

Lights have puzzled scientists for fifty years. The same story reports sightings of the lights in the days before the Civil War. They may be seen from as far away as Blowing Rock or the Old Yonahlosse Trail over Grandfather Mountain some fifteen miles distant from Brown Mountain. At some points closer to Brown Mountain, the lights seem as large as the balls of fire from a Roman candle.

In 1919 the question of the Brown Mountain Lights was brought to the attention of the Smithsonian Institution and the U. S. Weather Bureau. Dr. W. J. Humphries of the Weather Bureau investigated and reported that the Brown Mountain Lights were similar to the Andes Light of South America. The Andes Light and its possible relation to the Brown Mountain Lights became the topic of a paper read before the American Meterological Society in April 1941. In this report Dr. Herbert Lyman represented the lights as a manifestation similar to the Andes Light.

For countless centuries the Cherokee Indians watched the lights rising above the ridge of Brown Mountain, and another explanation was that the lights were the spirits of Indian maidens seeking their husbands and lovers

The Brown Mountain Lights.

killed in a great battle sometime around the year 1200.

But, perhaps, the most exciting explanation of all for the lights has been overlooked. In recent years the theory has been advanced that the mystery lights are UFOs and that this remote area is a gathering place for the flying saucers whose extraterrestrial beings use them to land and later take off after the visitors gather information about our planet.

What irony if, as we explore space seeking life on other planets, we are being observed and have been for centuries by the very beings we are attempting to contact through interplanetary travel and radio communication.

If you would like to see the lights for yourself, they are best observed on clear fall nights.

Perhaps this ancient mystery will one day be solved. Who knows what the answer will be!

THE CURSE OF THE EGYPTIAN TOMB

In the pleasant, quiet years before the Civil War it would seem that Anne Withers had everything to look forward to. Her father was a wealthy Georgetown, South Carolina, planter with a lovely home. He sent his daughter to the best schools and she became an accomplished linguist and musician.

All went happily until Anne and a handsome sea captain fell desperately in love. Her parents disapproved of the match, for they had hoped she would marry a young man from a Georgetown family whom they considered their social equal. But Anne was determined to marry the sea captain. Her only concession was to agree to her parents' request to postpone the marriage until after his next voyage. During that interval they hoped her affections might turn to one of the young men in Georgetown.

But, as the time arrived for the captain to

return, Anne was as steadfast as ever and there was nothing her parents could do but keep their promise. They ordered a lavish white satin wedding dress to be designed for her by the most outstanding dressmaker in Charleston. Her mother gave directions to the cooks to prepare a sumptuous wedding feast, and the fragrance of cakes baking and the aroma of smoking hams floated out into the air from the kitchen behind the big house.

Anne was happier than she had ever been in her life. Christopher Corbitt was not only a handsome man but kind and thoughtful as well. And what colorful adventures he related of far-away places. She was so bored with the talk of the young Georgetown planters about rice or indigo or their problems with slaves. Christopher never spoke of such drab matters. She listened to his stories enthralled.

The ribbons of her yellow muslin dress fluttered in the breeze as she stood one after-noon looking out over the blue waters of Winyah Bay. Surely, her captain's ship would be in soon. In her mind she pictured the dress she would wear when she greeted him. Of course, she would not be able to come down to the dock but would have to wait at her home for him to make a proper call.

The day before the wedding, Christopher Corbitt's boat sailed into port and within the hour he was calling at the Withers home. Anne's maid, Cindy, came to tell her he had arrived. Of course, she knew it, for she had been peeking from behind the curtain of her bedroom window. She came floating gracefully down the stairs in a full-skirted pink dress trimmed with white lace. The stair rail was festooned for the wedding with great ropes of green smilax leaves. What a beautiful sight Anne was to her captain!

She blushed as she looked at him, and for a moment neither could speak. They seated themselves in the big parlor at one side of the entrance hall and talked of the wedding arrangements. Then he began to tell her about his voyage. Stopping suddenly he said, "I almost forgot your gift. It is very rare and suitable only for you."

Captain Corbitt opened a small box and withdrew an exquisitely carved gold bracelet. It was made of tiny carved beetles with blazing ruby eyes, and the beetles were linked together by a delicate gold chain. Anne gazed at it in admiration. "How beautiful and unusual.

The carved golden bracelet.

I've never seen anything like it. Is it quite old?"

"Ah, there's an interesting story behind it. It came from the tomb of an Egyptian princess. At one of the ports on my voyage a rough-looking fellow approached me just as I was ready to board ship. He pulled at my sleeve and I thought he was about to ask for money for a pint of grog, but instead he showed me this bracelet. He said he had bought it from an old beggar in India, and from then on nothing but bad luck had followed him."

Anne looked at the bracelet dubiously. "Do you think it really is unlucky?"

"My dear, if I believed that, would I bring it to the person I love most in the world? No. The fellow was the cause of his own bad luck. He wanted the money to get to the nearest grog shop, for his eyes were bleary and I'm sure he had been drinking."

Anne tried to unfasten the clasp of the bracelet and put it on but could not. Christopher attempted to do it also, but it would not open.

"Never mind," said Anne. "Cindy is quite clever with her hands and she can unfasten it. I will wear it tomorrow night for the wedding. It is beautiful."

On the following night all the guests were assembled at the home of the bride. Captain Corbitt waited at the entrance hall for Anne. She appeared at the top of the steps and suddenly he heard her scream. One scream followed another and before he could reach her she had fallen headlong down the spiral stairway and lay at his feet. When he picked her

The tiny claws loosened their hold.

up she was dead. Around her wrist the tiny ruby eyes of the golden beetles glowed with a fiery light.

"Take the bracelet off. Take it off! It killed her," Cindy cried out. Corbitt leaned over and tore at the piece of jewelry. He was horrified to see that the beetles had fastened themselves into her wrist. As he removed it, the tiny claws loosened their hold and disappeared.

The Withers family sent the bracelet to a chemist in London. Soon a letter arrived with his report. Imbedded in each beetle were threadlike claws containing a deadly poison from the Orient. Anne had worn the bracelet only a few minutes when the warmth of her body released them.

For many years there have been reports that on moonlight nights a beautiful girl in a magnificent white bridal gown is seen walking on the porch and in the garden of the Withers-Powell house in Georgetown. It is said to be the ghost of Anne Withers felled by the curse of a bracelet bringing death from an Egyptian tomb.

RAILROAD BILL

Was the southern Robin Hood really a man named Morris Slater? Does his ghost still haunt the Alabama woods around the little cabins at Pine Grove, Elewy, and Nymph near the Louisville Railroad line?

There were no screens at the windows of the tiny, unpainted ramshackly house near the railroad tracks but old Aunt Elly was used to that. When the sun went down and the night's chill began to settle in, she went to each window and carefully hooked the wooden shutter. She fastened them not only to keep out the cold night air but also to keep out whatever else might be lurking in the darkness—whether man, beast, or spirit.

She banked the fire so she would have hot coals in the morning, although she didn't need them to start up the wood in the old iron stove for she had nothing to heat upon it. There was

Railroad Bill's train.

no money to buy food. Since she had become too old and crippled by arthritis to work she had received a small monthly welfare check, but toward the end of each month there was never enough left. This morning she had fried her last piece of fatback.

She was glad to crawl under the worn quilt on the iron bed and go to sleep, for that was the best way not to think about hunger. Before long she heard a shot ring out close by. A train's whistle began to emit desperate "toot, toots" and then she heard men's voices calling and hounds baying.

"Don' never hunt trouble," she thought as she lay there still as a shriveled little old log. "Bad enuf to be hongry. Don' have to go runnin' out to see what it's all about an' git put in de jail, too. Dat's what happens when po' folks gits in trouble."

About that time Aunt Elly felt the house shake. It sounded like somebody had come running and taken a long leap landing right on her back porch. She forgot the misery in her bones and was out of bed and at the back door before you could say scat. Next came a rattling and a clatter on the porch. She opened the door and there stood a tall man with a wide grin across his face. Then he was gone—a straight, broad-shouldered fellow racing across her yard toward the pine woods.

Scattered in front of the door were cans of food.

"God bless Railroad Bill," she said to herself looking out at the woods, and fast as she could she gathered every can, hurried into the house, and hid them under her bed. This done, Aunt Elly crawled back beneath the quilt. She did not have long to wait.

Soon she heard a pounding at her cabin door. It shook the shack from the roof to the floor. Aunt Elly got up and cracked the door. There stood the sheriff and a few men more.

"Tell me, Aunt Elly, have you seen Railroad Bill? He's robbed a train and he'll shoot to kill."

The old lady pretended she was scared to death.

"Oh, sheriff, keep dat man way from heah. He mighty bad fellah, an' I hope he don' come neah."

"Don't you worry, Aunt Elly. We'll get him this time shore. We brung along some bloodhounds. He won't bother us no more." He jumped down from the porch and called,

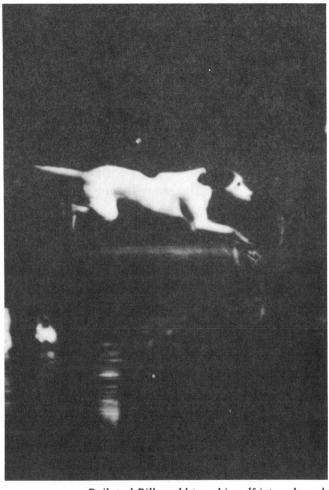

Railroad Bill could turn himself into a hound.

"Tell me, boys, did we bring three hounds or four? Seems to me we brought just three and now I see one more."

But no one paid it any mind and through the woods they went. The dogs were snuffling on the ground like they had got the scent. But they came right out on the other side—no Railroad Bill in sight—and the sheriff saw that the fourth hound dog had vanished in the night. The hair rose on the back of his neck as he turned to a friend and said, "That was no bloodhound that ran with our pack. That was Railroad Bill! He's led us on a merry chase. Now he's laughing in his bed."

For many years this Alabama bandit eluded the law. A Robin Hood, Railroad Bill continued to rob the freight trains along the Louisville and Nashville Railroad lines, distributing his loot among the poor. Some think the police finally caught him. Some think they never did. But many say the ghost of the tall man still haunts the pine woods near the tracks. And, when some poor family finds food outside their door, one of them is apt to look cautiously around for the law and then mutter, "God bless Railroad Bill."

GHOST OF
THE OLD FORT

Among the crumbling brick tombs and the
dark ruins of an old fort on Georgia's St.
Simons Island roams the restless spirit of one
of the South's most fascinating ghosts. Scholar,
missionary to the Indians, or madman? Who
can tell unless someday someone is able to
communicate with the apparition of Christian
Gottlieb Priber.

Christian Priber arrived in Charleston,
South Carolina, in 1736. He soon made friends
with the most cultivated people. His manners
were so fine and his conversation so scholarly
that he charmed the society of the day, and
they knew him as Dr. Priber. But one day Dr.
Priber and the handsome leather-bound chest
that held the manuscript of a book he was writing disappeared.

Within a few months rumors reached
Charleston that there was a man "speaking

many languages and learned in all sciences and arts" who had settled in the Smoky Mountains among the Cherokees. They heard that he was setting up a new government in the Cherokee nation. "There is some mistake," said they. "It can't be Dr. Priber."

A short while later an Indian runner arrived at the mansion of Goveror Bull of South Carolina. He carried a letter stating that a new country called the Republic of Paradise had been formed and that everyone not willing to become a citizen must leave the country at once! The epistle was signed, "Christian Priber, Prime Minister."

Government officials of the colonies of South Carolina and Georgia were astonished, and they decided that Priber should be captured and imprisoned at once. They thought that he was trying to set the Indians against the colonists.

It was not an easy task to capture the Prime Minister of Paradise. Men were sent to arrest him, but there were intercepted by the Indians and narrowly escaped losing their lives. Their scalps were saved only when Priber intervened. The men returned to relate an incredible story of meeting Priber who, they said, spoke Cherokee like a native, was married to an Indian maiden, and showed them a dictionary of the Cherokee language, which he had written. Priber made every effort to get them to join his country, which he told them was to be a place of perfect happiness. All property was to be held in common, there would be no poverty, and women had political equality with men.

In the spring of 1743 Priber felt it his duty to make peaceful overtures to the Creek Indians, so he set out with a guard of Cherokee braves and his manuscript in his wooden chest. But the English had learned of his intentions and captured him, taking him by boat to the prison barracks on St. Simons Island.

Even there he was given unusual privileges, and visitors arrived to talk with him on many subjects. Nothing is said in the records of how or when Priber died there in the barracks, nor has the book he was writing ever been discovered.

Some say, at night, when the mist rolls in from the water, voices can be heard near the barracks. There are those who think the language is Cherokee, others say it is German or Latin or even Spanish. Is it a coincidence that

Priber was an accomplished linguist? During the time he was in Charleston he was known to speak all of these languages fluently.

Surely, the ghost of the Prime Minister of Paradise could tell some interesting stories. It would be worth spending a night near the eerie ruins of the old fort just to listen.

THE GHOST OF ELIZABETH ROUTT

Would you like to meet the spirit of a beautiful woman walking in her bridal gown among the ruins of an Alabama mansion? You may want to learn more about the fair Elizabeth before you decide. In the early years of the last century near the small town of Hazel Green there was a fine house owned by Elizabeth Routt. She was lovely, auburn-haired, and, perhaps, fatal!

When Elizabeth was still quite young, the neighbors were invited to her wedding to the serious-minded Mr. Gibbons. Sadly, it was just a matter of months before her new husband became ill and died. A less-than-respectable period of mourning had elapsed before Mrs. Gibbons remarried. This time the bridegroom was a handsome Irishman named Flannigan who had curly black hair. Unfortunately, within the year he too was the victim of a sudden and undetermined illness.

It was not long before the tragic experiences of the young widow attracted the sympathy of Alexander Jeffries, a plantation owner who met her on one of his visits to the area. After a brief courtship, they married. They had lived together for several years when Mr. Jeffries' health began to decline. He too fell ill and died. His widow took over the management of the plantation and, it is said, "she ruled the slaves with an iron hand."

In 1839 Mrs. Jeffries wed a local legislator named Robert High of nearby Limestone County. Mrs. High turned over management of the property to her new husband, and for a time the pair seemed very happy together. But in 1842, much to the surprise of their neighbors, Mr. High suddenly became desperately ill. Within a week he was dead.

Soon afterward, Mrs. High met a New Market merchant named Absalom Brown who first offered his sympathy and then his heart. They married on March 16, 1846. Finally, it seemed all would go well for Elizabeth. The pair built a handsome home a mile east of Hazel Green, for Mrs. Brown longed to entertain the members of the prominent families of

Madison County. The house was so elaborate it took a slave and carpenter more than a year to build. Its furnishings were the finest obtainable.

Elizabeth presided at sumptuous candlelight dinners, and the house became the center of a constant round of parties. But a year after the couple had moved into their new home, Absalom Brown died in a most gruesome fashion. It was a slow and painful death, and his entire body was horribly swollen.

The night after his death, a parade of lanterns bobbed along in the darkness as slaves carried the casket to the family graveyard. A few friends watched despite the rain and wind as the body was lowered into the grave. Elizabeth Brown had insisted that Absalom be buried immediately, saying that the appearance of her husband was such that a public funeral would only serve to make the occasion more tragic.

This time there was much gossip in the small community of Hazel Green, but no one dared voice any suspicions to the widow. Less than a year had passed before Mrs. Brown was on her way to the altar once more. On a warm May afternoon she married a man named

*The ghost of
Elizabeth Routt.*

Willis Routt. Misfortune struck once more and before the pair could celebrate their first anniversary, Elizabeth's sixth husband died!

Adjacent to the Routt plantation was the property of Abner Tate, a man who appeared immune to her charms. It was not long before quarrels began to erupt between Tate and Mrs. Routt. Finally, Tate decided to visit her home and talk with the widow about her livestock, which frequently wandered over onto his property and did considerable damage. Elizabeth did not invite him into the parlor, and as the pair stood arguing in the large center hall, he happened to glance at the hat rack near the door. Upon it Tate saw the hats of six men, and he was shocked to recognize each hat as belonging to one of her husbands.

Tate was now convinced that she had murdered the men and that the hat rack was evidence of her foul deeds. He formally charged her with murder, but there was no concrete evidence to substantiate the charges and the case was dropped. Soon afterward, at dusk in his own yard, Abner Tate was struck down by a shotgun blast to the stomach. The shotgun had been fired by a slave, and the slave was killed before he could make a statement. Tate was certain Mrs. Routt had hired the slave to kill him in an attempt at vengeance.

Not long afterward a suitor of the widow accused Tate of murdering a trader and burning his body in the fireplace. He charged him with the man's murder, but Tate was acquitted. Filled with anger, he wrote a pamphlet calling Elizabeth Routt a female Bluebeard around whose bed the ghosts of her dead husbands nightly assembled. Mrs. Routt moved to Mississippi.

After that the candles no longer shone through the windows of the Routt house. It became a gray, ramshackle monstrosity and today only the ruins are still there. The graveyard is overgrown, its tombstones clutched by twisting vines, and at night they say that the fair Elizabeth walks there in her bridal gown surrounded by six vaporous, fleshless forms—each the ghost of a husband who once received her kiss of death.

THE GHOST ON PARK ROAD

Amy and John MacLeod moved into the red brick house on Park Road in October of 1962. The house was about thirty-five years old, set in the midst of a large tree-shaded lot, and although it was homey looking, the architecture was nondescript.

"We had lived in it for about a month when the first thing happened that let us know something was wrong," said Amy. "I was in the kitchen, and the door to the basement where our dog stayed was open. Suddenly, I heard someone whistling a tune. The dog began to bark fiercely and I called him upstairs, but he wouldn't come. He just stayed down there and kept barking.

"I grew very frightened because the whistling continued, and I knew there couldn't be anyone down there. The German Shepherd barked as if he would bark his lungs out, and

I thought of calling the police but something told me not to do it. This is not a natural thing, I decided, and if they come out here and find no one, they will think I am crazy.

"John called at noon and I told him something very odd was going on in the basement. He was awestruck. After a while the whistling stopped and I got up enough courage to go down. No one was there, absolutely no one.

"Then the strangest thing of all happened. I don't know whether you have ever felt a strong compulsion from outside yourself, but one day in January when the children were small, I wanted to go to the store. My son said, 'I can't find my shoes, Mommy.' We looked in his room but they were not there. We looked everywhere we could think of in the house. Then we went out to the sandpile, but they weren't there either.

"All the time something was telling me, this child doesn't know where those shoes are and we are not going to find them by any ordinary means.

"I had the strangest impulse to unlock the door to the attic. We had closed it off because it was dangerous for the children. I walked up the steep stairs unconsciously counting each

step. They were not sealed and there were bare
studs with a hole by each riser. About half-
way up I turned and went back down, got a
coat hanger and straightened it out. I went back
up to the thirteenth step and I put the coat
hanger down in the hole.

"Probing around with it I pulled up first
one shoe and then the other. While I was fish-
ing them out I knew very well that wasn't all
that was in that hole. Still under the power of
this strong subconscious urge, I went back
downstairs, brought the vacuum cleaner up and
put the hose down into the hole. The first thing
that came up was a death certificate.

"There were insurance receipts for
$25,000, a note that had been pinned to the
body at a funeral home giving instructions to
the undertaker, and an envelope that had held
a man's rings and poems written by a woman
in grief. I was certain they had all been deliberately placed in this hole to be found at some
later date.

"According to the death certificate, the
man had died on July 13, 1960, of a ruptured
cervical vertebra. From then on I believed that
there was something connecting his death to
the things that were happening in the house,

and that finding the child's shoes in that hole had been for a purpose. To this day I cannot say how they got there.

"I wondered about the purpose of this act until I nearly went insane. The interesting thing was that the wife had taken this man's insurance money, bought this house a few weeks after his death, and married another man almost instantly. I never met her. A lawyer closed the sale when we bought the house, but somehow I continued to wonder about her. She came back once to see me, but I was not there. What could she have wanted to say?

"Last fall I found out how the man died. He was only thirty years old and had a good job. It was three o'clock in the morning and he was driving alone on a straight stretch of highway. He was going a hundred miles an hour. The tanker in front of him saw him coming in his rearview mirror and pulled off the road onto the shoulder in order to avoid being hit. But the man veered off onto the shoulder also and deliberately rammed the tanker from behind. Did he commit suicide or did something kill him? Did something deliberately turn that wheel?

"Our whole family knew there was a very

frightening atmosphere in this house. John and I had the attic insulated and floored and a big dormitory room made up there for the children. At least we were getting rid of the attic as a dark, ominous sort of place. We painted it a cheerful color and placed the children's three beds in a row. It was an enormous room and we bought a huge hooked rug about twelve by eighteen feet for the floor.

"But we were only deceiving ourselves, and in a way we knew it. One night right after we moved them up there, John and I woke up at the same time and sat straight up in bed. John said, 'There's a man walking upstairs.' There were big feet stomping across the floor—*boom, boom, boom*—right over our heads, and we could hear it when it came to the rug, walked across it, and then stepped off. We were petrified. We jumped up and I reached over on the nightstand and got a jar of cream and handed it to John saying, 'Here. This is at least something to hit it with.' Then I went into the kitchen in the dark and got a butcher knife, and we went up those steps. When we turned on the light there was not a soul there and the children were dead to the world. You can tell when children are asleep, you know.

"We went down to the basement, got the dog and took him upstairs, but when we reached the steps leading to the second floor, he wouldn't budge. He laid his ears back, rolled his eyes, and the hair stood up on the back of his neck. We held him by the collar and dragged him up those stairs and I thought he would die of fright. About a year later the dog did die, very young, and the veterinarian couldn't find anything wrong. I believe the dog was just frightened to death.

"After that incident 'it' became very brave and would come and knock on the walls by the bed and the ceiling right over our heads. The most distressing thing about this was that it seemed to be from my side of the wall rather than the other side, and this produced the most terrible sense of fear, for there was no doubt that it was right in the room with me. One night it began to play with my hair, taking its fingers and running them through it all.

"Sometimes we could hear it knock on the door to the bedroom and the door would slowly open. The manifestations were numerous and incredible. I've heard people say that children cause these things. The children could not have caused them, but the children understood it.

"One night as we were in the car preparing to leave for church John said, 'Let me go back and turn on the porch light so it won't be dark when we come home.' One of the children said, 'It's no use, Daddy. When we come back it will be off.' John got out and turned it on from the inside anyway. When we returned, the porch was in darkness. Lights often went on and off, particularly at night if we were talking about it. I remember a night, one of the few times I told a friend about the occurrences, while we were talking the lights went on and off and on and off.

"I wouldn't have spent the night alone in that house if my life had depended upon it. The worst siege we ever had with it was when I was working at night and would come in late and sit down with a cup of tea to read the paper. I had just settled myself with my paper and cup of tea one night when I heard a *knock, knock, knock* right beside me on the table. Looking up, I saw a gray vapor hovering over me. Then it dissipated.

"Another night I panicked badly. Again, I was sitting at the dining room table. There was a closet door in the room that did not shut

The light on the porch blinked off.

tightly. Abruptly, a loud knock came and then a sharp crash as if the thing had kicked the door with all its might. The door began to bounce back and forth and back and forth, and I began screaming. My husband came running from the bedroom and said, 'What in the world was that?' 'The thing kicked the door,' I answered.

"One night when I knew my husband would be gone, I asked my oldest boy to wait up for me. He met me at the door, his face filled with fright. 'Mother, that thing has been knocking all evening. I'm really wondering if it is going to try to harm you or something.' And it did seem to single me out more than other members of the family. I said, 'Let's sit down here and keep all the lights on and see if anything else happens.' There was a hall-way that led from the dining room across the back of the house. I sat rocking and waiting, and my son sat on the sofa.

"It was not long before we heard heavy footsteps starting out from the dining room and moving the length of that hall. The mysterious visitor came in the room and walked right up to where I was sitting. I jumped out of that chair and said, 'Jimmy, I'm scared to death!'

and he said, 'Momma, don't worry. God, will take care of you.'

"During all of this my husband and I very badly wanted to move but could not afford it. We had bought the house for an unbelievably low price. The payments were small, and it was convenient to our work.

"That summer someone else encountered our ghost in a most uncanny way. A friend came over to spend the night while her husband was away, and I gave her my bedroom. I went into the next room and dozed off lying on the sofa. I had just closed my eyes when I was startled awake by a knocking on the piano lid in the room on the other side of me, and I thought, 'Oh my, what is going to happen next?' For this is the way it often started. But I heard no more. A little while passed and then a sound came from my friend in the next room. The light went on and I heard her get up. Finally the light went off. The next morning I rose early to find her already up and dressed.

"'Who got in bed with me last night?' she asked. And I said, 'Did someone get in bed with you?' 'He certainly did,' she replied, 'and whoever it was was cold as ice.' It was mid-

July and the house was not air conditioned. 'He lay right up next to me. I ran my hand down the bed and I could feel the pressure beside me, but I couldn't feel anyone. Once it seemed to be lying across my legs and I couldn't move. It was terrifying.'

"I told her the same thing had happened to me, and it was dreadful to feel that thing beside me and feel the weight of it upon the bed. I was petrified and yet curious, for I was convinced that, somehow, it was trying to communicate with me. To this day I shall never know what it was trying to say.

"The happiest day of my life was the day we moved. I stood in the driveway at dusk and looked back at the house. We had left the porch light on, for there were a few things to pick up the next day and we didn't want the house to appear empty.

"Do you know that as I stood there the light on the porch blinked off and on twice—then went out."

PHANTOM RIDER OF THE SHENANDOAH

Jeremy Forest did not know why he had awakened in the middle of the night. He only knew he was wide awake and filled with a strange sense of excitement. He could not have gone back to sleep if he had tried.

Getting up, he pulled on his jeans and threw a jacket over his pajama top. He opened the front door and stepped outside, closing the door gently behind him. Something was tugging at Jeremy with the irresistible pull of a magnet. But, what?

For a moment the boy stood on the porch of the old Virginia farmhouse where he was visiting his grandparents in the Shenandoah Valley. Then, as if propelled by some force beyond his control, he found himself walking through the yard, down the hill, and toward the road below the house. Silhouetted by moonlight, gnarled black limbs of ancient oaks implored an impassive sky.

As the fifteen-year-old boy stood beside the road he heard a faint clatter in the distance. The sound grew closer by the moment. Hoofbeats—the hoofbeats of a horse, seldom felt by this blacktop road in the 1970s. Years back it had been a narrow trail for stagecoaches, then a plank road, and now macadam used by farmers. It wound and curved through the Shenandoah Valley from Martinsburg, Virginia, toward Richmond.

Jeremy waited with some apprehension, for what rider could be galloping along the deserted road at this hour of the night? Suddenly a horse and rider rose rapidly over the crest of the small hill from the direction of Martinsburg. Jeremy shrunk back into the brush beside the road, hoping to remain unseen. But the horse and rider pulled to an abrupt halt directly before him. There was a luminous, unearthly glow about them in the darkness.

"Is this the way to Richmond?" called the rider. Astonished, Jeremy realized it was the voice of a woman. He stepped toward the road and looked into the face of the rider—a lovely girl with long blond braids.

"Would you ride behind me? I am not sure

The gnarled black limbs of ancient trees implored an impassive sky.

I can find my way alone," she said. Jeremy hesitated. What would his grandparents think if they awoke and found him gone? But again a strange compulsion, the same one that had awakened him and caused him to leave the house, seemed to take away his will to resist.

Jeremy threw himself over the back of the horse behind her.

"Why are you going to Richmond?" he asked.

"To warn Gen. Stonewall Jackson," she replied.

"Warn Jackson?" he repeated bewildered.

"Of course. I must let him know the Yankees are heading toward Richmond planning to trap him and his men," said the girl.

Patches of mist lay along the road as they galloped through the mountains of the Shenandoah Valley, but the horse never faltered, never slowed its pace.

It was not long before they saw Union campfires flickering ahead in the darkness. A blue-coated picket, with rifle pointed, stepped into the road before them. Jeremy's heart gave a bump in his chest.

"Halt! Who goes there?"

"A friend of the Union," the girl replied.

"Pass on," said the picket. Much to Jeremy's relief they were on their way through the lines and past the camp.

Surrounded by the dark shadows of the night, they galloped across a river that shone black in the moonlight, while water splashed about the horse's feet. Voices floated up from among the trees along the riverbank. Sparks flew high in the night air, and Jeremy knew it must be another Union encampment. He saw the ring of campfires, the shadowy outline of tents and wagons.

"Halt!" shouted a sentry. The girl took some papers from beneath her cape and flashed them quickly before the sentry. They were the passes she had been given by Confederate soldiers allowed to return south as part of a prisoner exchange.

"We're on our way to Richmond to join relatives," she said.

The sentry glanced at them perfunctorily, looked up at the girl admiringly, and started to tell them to pass. But giving her credentials a second glance he frowned. At that moment she spurred her horse, which gave one mighty leap and dashed into the darkness. Shots rang out behind them. He heard men shouting and horses whinnying. Then came the pound of pursuing hooves, and he suddenly felt they were after *him*. He screamed into the blackness but the wind flung the scream back into his face. The girl's horse galloped valiantly, and it seemed as though they were hurtling headlong into the deepest darkness he had ever known.

Jeremy wished he was back in his bed at his grandparents' house. Anywhere, in fact, but on this terrifying ride.

"How close are they?" asked the girl turning her head.

"How close?" she repeated urgently.

The boy looked back and saw horses and riders with mangled, twisted, screaming white faces almost upon them. Suddenly, she reined her horse sharply to the right. Branches struck Jeremy's face, tore at his shirt, while on either side of him the forest flowed past. He pressed his face hard against her back and closed his eyes. When he had the courage to look once more he saw they were on a narrow path, and at that moment there appeared a man dressed in black, astride a huge white horse.

"Ashby. Turner Ashby. At your service, ma'am. What have we here?" he asked in a

The Phantom Rider.

cool, confident voice looking from the girl to Jeremy. Ashby was one of Stonewall Jackson's most trusted and daring scouts.

"I did not want to ride alone, and I summoned him to come with me," said she. Colonel Ashby reined in his horse close to hers, and as she leaned over to speak with him, a long blond braid fell from the hood of her cape.

"General Banks knows General Jackson's position and is planning to trap him and his troops, Colonel Ashby."

"And you are—?"

"I am Belle Boyd."

Colonel Ashby dismounted. His black cloak seemed to become part of the night itself. Only his face gleamed white in the darkness as he qave her his most dashing smile.

"It is a great privilege to meet the young lady of whom I have heard so much. I will convey your message to Jackson myself."

With that he leaped upon his white horse and like a flash of light both horse and rider disappeared into the night.

Belle Boyd. Belle Boyd—Jeremy wondered where he had heard her name. Then he remembered. She was the greatest woman Confederate spy of all. By now she had wheeled her horse about, and away they galloped. Over the narrow path and back to the road. Jeremy's arms clung tight about her waist. A strong wind came up and blew her cape back around him. Then the crash of thunder rolled away in the distance like far-off cannon fire. Jeremy felt drops of rain begin to pelt his face. On they rode and the boy became soaked to the skin. He was so exhausted he felt he could not hold out much longer, and his chilled hands began to slip and lose their grip.

Once more he heard the sound of horses whinnying and pursuing hoofs. He turned to see the horrible white faces straining to catch up with them in the darkness. The girl spurred her horse and as she did so, Jeremy was thrown from the horse and fell to the ground. All he knew was that he must get out of the way of the riders following Belle Boyd. They were almost upon him before he was able to roll to one side. In a flash of lightning he saw them pass, but not one ever looked his way. After that the boy remembered no more.

The following morning when he awoke in his own bed, his face was scratched, his clothes wet, and his shoes muddy. Quickly he ran outside. When he returned to the house, his grandmother noticed his appearance and gave him an odd look. He told her he had slipped and fallen.

"Well, boy, you had better hurry and get some dry clothes on. What a sight you are!" she said.

He saw himself in the mirror of the big walnut bureau with its white marble top. The events of the night were beginning to come back to him. He recalled the story his grand-

mother had told him long ago of the beautiful
Belle Boyd and how she had ridden to warn
Stonewall Jackson. Jeremy knew it must be
true. For hadn't he seen the campfires glow-
ing, the sentries calling "Halt!" in the night,
the dashing Colonel Ashby—and Belle Boyd
herself?

How had it happened? Jeremy Forest
would never know.

THE GHOST OF
MARSE JOEL

Joel Cloud built his house on Childress Creek a mile or two from Georgia's old Wrightsboro–to–Washington stagecoach road. Beside the water he constructed a large grist mill, and farmers from miles around brought their grain. As the mill prospered Joel invested in land, and each day he would ride over his acreage in a buggy to inspect his crops.

His home of sun-cured, handmade brick was a comfortable one-story dwelling in which he raised a family and lived for thirty years. When he died in 1861 he was buried in the garden beside the house.

He willed his property to his son, Obadiah, who was a highly respected young man in the community and a representative to the state legislature. When Obadiah decided to add a second story to the old home he was amazed to discover forty thousand dollars in gold hid-

den among the rafters of the original roof. With
the gold he found a note from his father saying, "More buried in the garden."

Obadiah, or Little Obie as he was called,
dug in every spot he could think of looking
for the gold. Late one night he sat gazing out
his parlor window at the yard in the moonlight thinking about the gold. This room had
once been Joel Cloud's bedroom and Obadiah
wondered if his father had buried the gold
within sight of this very window.

As he looked out he was astonished to see
an old buggy drawn by a black horse travel-
ing along the edge of the field. He must have
seen that buggy a thousand times in his youth,
for it was the one his father had driven as he
went about the farm overseeing his land.
Obadiah dashed out of the house, but by the
time he reached the field the wagon was no-
where in sight. The next morning he awoke
certain it had all been a dream, but he walked
out to the field just the same. There in the
plowed ground he found the fresh tracks of
wagon wheels. This was not the only time he
is said to have seen the ghostly wagon. He died
in 1920 without ever finding the buried money
and the house was abandoned.

The story of the buried gold has not been forgotten in the area, and the land has been combed with metal detectors. There is hardly a boy in Wrightsboro who has not dug for it.

Those who have been there at night and chanced to see the buggy and the black horse have left hurriedly. Braver souls swear they would stay, and that the person with courage to follow the wraith of the buggy will meet Joel Cloud who will lead them to the treasure.

SPECTER OF THE SORREL STALLION

For centuries wild ponies roamed the off-shore islands of Georgia, and many were the attempts to capture them and take them to the mainland. But the men trying to round them up failed, for the ponies had a mysterious protector. Always a handsome sorrel stallion would appear and keep the horses together herding them away from the catchers.

And if the catchers were lucky enough to pen any of the ponies, the stallion was clever enough somehow to set them free. On one drive he kept the catchers guessing continually until after several weeks they left in disgust without capturing a horse.

A fascinating story has been told of how a Spanish Arabian stallion in the possession of loyalist Julian Leavett was seized by the patriots. Escaping from his captors, the strong and intelligent animal swam out to one of the islands. But, however the horse may have gotten there, it is a fact that such a stallion lived on the islands. He was a large chestnut sorrel with a golden mane and tail, and he galloped as if carried along by the wind. No one was ever able to catch and pen him, although many tried, and he swam from one island to another.

In the fall of 1880 two men went out to St. Catherine's Island to try their hand at penning some of the horses. They tried for almost a week and finally were able to pen a dozen of the ponies.

"These horses are not like most of the wild ponies you see," the older drover said to the younger. "They are larger and stronger and smarter."

"I've found that out," his companion exclaimed. "The old stallion must have died long ago. Why haven't the ponies been rounded up and brought to the mainland by now?"

"I don't rightly know," replied the older man. "Of course, the old stallion died. He was never seen in the daytime and although no one ever found him they thought he swam out to sea. He no longer galloped up and herded the ponies away, but they say he would come at night and tear the pens and the ponies would scatter all over the island."

"Did they see or hear him?"

"Never while he was doing it, but afterward they would see him in the moonlight and they knew it was no real horse they were watching, for they could see right through him."

"It was a ghost horse then?"

"Yes, and no one wanted to go after ponies guarded by a ghost, so for years they've been left to themselves. I wouldn't be out here tonight if I hadn't been offered a good price to bring some of them in to the mainland." The old drover pulled his beard thoughtfully, placed his clay pipe on the ground beside him, and began to unroll his blanket.

"In the morning the barge will be here and we must have the ponies ready," he said looking over toward the pen. "Now, we'd better get some rest."

Shortly after midnight, the old drover, who slept lightly as outdoorsmen do, awoke. He had heard a sound nearby and he raised himself on one elbow to listen. Now, it came again. It was the noise of boards ripping and snapping and then the pounding of hooves. He jumped up and ran toward the pen, but he was too late.

In the moonlight he watched the marsh ponies galloping off into the scrub that covered the center of the island. The young man joined him holding one of their saddle horses that had broken loose. The animal was trembling with fright.

"Leave the horse. He won't go anywhere," said the drover and he walked around to the far side of the pen with the younger man. There, beside a post, were the boards lying upon the ground—the ends with the nails torn and split. The older man shook his head as he picked up a board and looked at it.

"Maybe they began fighting and fell against it," volunteered his helper. But neither

really believed it, for the pen had been strongly
built to prevent that very thing from happening. As they stood dismayed and bewildered
they heard a floating, resonant call in the distance. More than anything, it was like the soft,
plaintive call of a stallion to his mare. It might
almost have been the wind, but it was not.

From behind the undulating dunes of sand
and onto the moonlit beach walked a shining
copper-colored stallion, his feet stepping
proudly as if he were on parade. The two men
watched silently, hypotized by the animal's su-
perb form and grace. Elegantly the stallion
placed his feet in the surf. For a moment he
looked back at the dunes emitting an exultant,
full-throated sound and then with head held
high, he began to walk out into the surf along
the moonlit path that led from the shore across
the water.

A strong wind came up and the waves
grew higher, but he walked on, breasting them
with his powerful shoulders and continuing to
rise above the crest until a tremendous wave
lifted him so high he appeared to stand upon
the very surface of the water. At that moment
a cloud obscured the moon and all was darkness. When the shimmering silver path reap-

peared upon the water, the stallion was gone.

Reports continued of strange, seemingly impossible escapes by island ponies. Always, they happened at night, and many claimed to have seen the phantom stallion but few gave as credible a description as the two drovers— although, they never went back to round up the wild ponies again.

THE GIRL ON
THE ROCK AT
TOCCOA FALLS

Why is the outline of the figure of a girl seen on the wet rock beside beautiful Toccoa Falls in northern Georgia? Early settlers looked at it and marveled. A story in Indian lore may explain why it is here, but how? Ah, that is another matter. . . .

Before the invasion by European settlers the Cherokees were a powerful tribe. They inhabited Kentucky, Tennessee, and parts of Virginia, South Carolina, Alabama, and Georgia. Warfare with other tribes, particularly the Creeks to the south, was common, but sometimes disputes over hunting grounds were settled by meetings between two warring tribes' chiefs and medicine men.

It is said that on one of these occasions the Cherokees sat in council with the Creeks for many days to arrange terms for an ex-

Toccoa Falls.

change of territory. There were numerous for-
malities to be observed, and at first it was po-
lite simply to sit in complete silence. Soon, the
didahnvwisgi, or medicine man, would recite
a long prayer. This was followed by the pipe
ceremony, and the pipe was passed to each
member of the council. Then came long and
elaborate speeches of greeting and the presen-
tation of gifts.

The Creeks had prepared a fine feast,
which was served by the young girls. The most
beautiful of these girls was Morning Flower,
daughter of the Creek war chief. A Cherokee
brave called Sanuwa, son of a chief, was much
attracted to Morning Flower, and on long af-
ternoons while the chiefs were engaging in pre-
liminary courtesies, the pair began to meet at
the waterfall not far from the camp.

Sanuwa talked to Morning Flower of his
homeland where the purple mountains touched
the sky. They wandered together through the
forest as autumn leaves turned bronze and gold,
and joy and tenderness sprang up between
them. One beautiful blue-sky day Sanuwa
pointed out two eagles soaring above them spi-
raling in wild and silent flight, a male and female, free and beautiful. "I would like for us

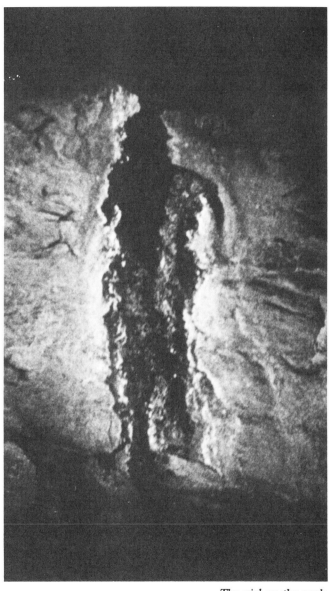

The girl on the rock.

to be like that pair of eagles for the rest of our lives," he told the girl.

He knew that he was expected to marry someone of a neighboring Cherokee clan to strengthen tribal ties, and Morning Flower was promised to a Creek warrior who had spoken to her father. But their hearts were not obedient to the wishes of their people.

As the ceremonies drew to a close, the Cherokees agreed to move back a day's walk to allow for the expansion of the other trible. The time had arrived for Sanuwa to return to the mountains with his father and the council members. He had made up his mind that he would leave with the others, but he asked Morning Flower to wait by the falls and promised he would come back for her the following evening to take her with him.

They were unable to say goodbye the next morning, but late that afternoon she went to the rock near the waterfall where he had asked her to wait. Morning Flower stayed until long after the sun had set behind the horizon and darkness had fallen. But late that night after the moon had gone down her tears began to flow.

Finally, she turned and in her pain and anguish walked deliberately into the falls. Within seconds the thundering force of the water had carried her over it down upon the rocks below into a deep pool beneath the plumy, white cascades.

It was almost daybreak when Sanuwa was finally able to make his way back. He called Morning Flower but there was no answer. Grief-stricken, he threw himself upon the ground. When the sun rose he went down to the foot of the falls. Looking up he saw the outline of his sweetheart, wet upon the face of the rock, and he knew in his heart what had happened.

Today, the form of Morning Flower may still be seen imprinted beside the falls. Students of ghosts are familiar with the shadows of hanged men—men who died protesting their innocence, only later to appear on courthouse walls. These shadows, no one has ever been able to erase or paint over. Faces of those who have died from violence or grief continue to be seen staring from the windows of certain houses.

And, even stone may bear the image of a heartbroken girl.

INDEX

M
MacLeod, Amy and
  John, 44–54
Martinsburg, Virginia, 56
Morning Flower, 76–79
Mulryne, John, 1

N
North Carolina
  Brown Mountain
    Lights, 15–20
  Charlotte's Van
    Landingham ghost,
    11–14
Nymph, Alabama, 28

O
Old Yonahlosse Trail, 18

P
Paradise, Republic of,
  35–37
Park Road ghost, 44–54
Pine Grove, Alabama, 28
Plains, Georgia, haunted
  house in, 6–10
Ponies, Georgia's wild,
  68–73
Priber, Christian
  Gottlieb, 34–37

Q

R
Railroad Bill, 28–33
Republic of Paradise, 35–
  37

Richmond, Virginia, 56
Robin Hood, 28, 33
Routt, Elizabeth, 38–43
Routt, Willis, 41–42

S
St. Catherine's Island,
  Georgia, 68–73
St. Simons Island,
  Georgia, 34–37
Sanuwa, 76–79
Savannah, Georgia
  Bonaventure Cemetery,
    1–5
  eternal dinner party in,
    1–6
Shenandoah Valley,
  phantom rider of the,
  55–64
Slater, Morris, 28–33
Smithsonian Institution,
  19
Smoky Mountains, 35
South Carolina
  Charleston, Dr. Priber
    and Republic of
    Paradise, 34–43
  Georgetown, and curse
    of the Egyptian tomb,
    21–27

T
Tate, Abner, 42–43
Tattnall, Josiah, 1–2
Tattnall, Josiah, Jr., 2–5
Tattnall, Mary, 1–2
Toccoa Falls, 74–79

ABOUT THE AUTHOR:

With more than twenty books to her credit,
NANCY ROBERTS continues to delight read-
ers, young and old, with her ghost stories and
southern folklore. Ms. Roberts teaches classes
in creative writing and is a popular speaker and
guest at schools, libraries, and bookstores. She
leads a busy life with her husband Jim Brown
in Charlotte, North Carolina.

OTHER BOOKS BY NANCY ROBERTS:

America's Most Haunted Places
Blackbeard and Other Pirates of the Atlantic Coast
Ghosts and Specters of the Old South
Civil War Ghosts and Legends
Ghosts of the Carolinas
Ghosts of the Southern Mountains and Appalachia
The Gold Seekers
Haunted Houses
North Carolina Ghosts
South Carolina Ghosts
This Haunted Southland

Southern
Ghosts